Excelling With
Excel Formulas

Rick Saldan

ALSO BY RICK SALDAN

Motivational Magic: Secrets for Accomplishing the Impossible

Breaking Free of the Matrix

Spiritual Influences on Classic Literature

Cold War Essays on Societal Breakdown

Correcting Corrections

Manchurian Candidates: Fact or Fiction

Lupus, The Disease With A Thousand Faces

Confronting Racial Hatred With Classic Literature

*Using Theatrical Stage Magic to
Assess Cognitive Development*

Let's Make Toastmasters Great Again

Excelling With Excel Formulas

How I Used Nested If-Then Loops and
Vlookups to Accomplish The Impossible

Rick Saldan

MOTIVATIONAL MAGIC

DEDICATION

To the many number crunchers who have toiled for hours working feverishly to achieve the impossible on their massive spreadsheets. To those who have lived inside of an electronic world seeking to tame and master its often beguiling and perplexing intricacies that stretch your mind so much it makes your brain feel like it is on fire. To those who have persevered and risen above these towering walls to hunt for and nail down the elusive solutions that they just somehow knew they could achieve if only they did not faint with weariness.

CONTENTS

CHAPTER ONE

The Mission Objective

I love Excel formulas. I love the complexity and intricacy. The more difficult and mind bending the scenario, the more I love to sink my teeth into the problem and figure out some way to solve it.

Such was the case with this problem. I was asked by a fund manager if it could be solved. Two partners in the bonds department of this financial firm told me they had worked on it off and on for 3 years and it was impossible to do this work with Excel. Impossible, you say? Oh, boy, that really perked my ears. This problem was out of the scope of what I was being paid to do for this financial firm and the gentleman I reported to told me that if I wanted to work on it, it would have to be after hours on my own time. The firm would not pay for it. I was also told a large international consulting firm had been retained at the hefty fee of $60,000, and they finally concluded it could not be done. After hearing that, I became super determined to try to resolve it and figure out a way to make it happen with Excel.

It's like a puzzle that eats away at you. You have a gut feeling it can be done and you have several ideas for how to approach it, but yet you are not really truly sure you can do it. It's a gamble. With so many big guns saying no it is impossible, then you really don't look too bad if you fail in your endeavor. On the other hand, if you can pull it off and bring it together, you look like a miracle worker. No, you don't just look like a miracle worker, you are a miracle worker. And that was the reputation that I wanted to work hard to earn at this firm. Someone known for working miracles and doing what others said was impossible.

I agreed to take on the project. I had to do it for free and the firm would not pay me for it. The only thing I asked this fund manager for was a glowing letter of recommendation if I could solve it.

I spent the next six weeks after hours, toiling away late into the midnight hours trying to crack the code. Even during the day, when I was not allowed to work on it, my mind was still trying different approaches to make it work. Kind of like a Rubik's Cube. You try one combination after another. When that fails, you trying a different set of steps and see if that works. You get closer and closer. A few sides of the Rubik's Cube have been unified and are all one color. That now gives you extra momentum to push harder and keep on pushing.

You get closer and closer. Now it becomes an absolute obsession. You must solve it. As the days go on, the fatigue of the undertaking starts to weigh heavy on you. You can't think as clearly as you did when you first started.

Now it takes more effort to move forward and you start to get lost in your thoughts. Like climbing a mountain where the higher you get in altitude, the more difficult it becomes for your body to function. Breathing is more laborious. Each step you take forward requires more concentration and more effort. That's exactly hw I would describe the six weeks it took to solve this.

You have to be a real Excel geek to totally appreciate everything written here. If you are an Excel novice, you'll read these pages and ask yourself, "What in the world is this guy talking about?" But if you love Excel like I love Excel, some of the insights and strategies in this book will be pure gold for you. If you have discovered some methods for making Excel do things others have said cannot be done, please reach out to me. I'd love to hear your story!

Bon Appetit!

Mission Objective: find the Rate of Return for the Bond Debenture Fund over a period of 20 months. Provide the fund manager with a High Yield Performance Extraction.

He provides us with two files, the Bond Holdings file and the Bond Trades file. To simplify the complexity of our numerous Vlookup formulas, we can copy the copy the Bond_Trades file onto the second tab of the Bond_Holdings file.

<u>Bond Holdings File</u>:

ME Date	March 31
Cusip	9999999$A
Issuer	Republic of Argentina
Coupon	5.250
S&P	BB
Moody	B1
LA Rating	--

Owned	10,000,000.000
Market Value	$6,425,000.00
Accrued Income	$ --
Total Value	$6,425,000.00
Security Type	Corporate

Bond Trades File:

Trade Date	March 31
Settlement	April 3
Cusip	498904AB7
Issuer Description	Knoll Inc.
P or S	S
Units Traded	16,500.00
Trade Price	108.625
First Money	$1,792,312.50
Interest Traded	$8,971.88
FirstMoney+Interest	$1,801,284.38
P/L	$116,062.50
Type Of Security	Corporate

Combine the Files into one Workbook

Goal: We will be using several Vlookup functions throughout. To simplify the complexity of our numerous Vlookup formulas, we can copy the copy the Bond_Trades file onto the second tab of the Bond_Holdings file.

Actions:

In the Bond_Holdings file,

Right click on the High Yield tab

4

The Mission Objective

Click Insert

Select Worksheet, click OK

Recommended: change the name of this new tab to "Trades" (right click)

Recommended: move this after the high yield tab

Recommended: change the name of the high yield tab to be "Holdings"

Go to the Bond_Trades file, copy and paste this to the new Trades tab

To avoid confusion later, we will still refer to each of these sheets as "Bond_Holdings" and "Bond_Trades."

CHAPTER TWO

Create a Unique Key Code and Previous Month Code

Our goal is to cross compare the records in the Holdings file against the Trades file. One a <u>monthly</u> basis, identify the those recordings in holdings which have a trade and those which do not.

In both files, create a Unique Key Code for each security that is different each month. Our Unique Key Code will be a combination of: cusip + month + year. We will use the "ME Date" from the Bond_Holdings file, and the "Trade Date" from the Bond_Trades file.

Because vlookups will be working with this field, the Unique Key Code must be in the first column (the vlookup feature does not function unless setup this way).

At this point, we see that the ME Dates and the Trade Dates are in the format of day-month-year. We will need to convert this to month-year prior to create our Unique Key Code.

Actions:

> Insert 3 columns. In the second, put in a month-year version of the ME Date. In the third column, put in a similar date, but for the previous month (by subtracting 31 days from the ME Date). We will use

this previous month code for several of the ROR formulas in later steps.

Pull up the Bond_Holdings sheet

Insert three columns at the far left, A, B and C

In A1, type the label "Key Code"

In B1, type the label "Date Code"

In C1, type the label "Prev Date Code"

In B2, type in the formula
        = TEXT(D2, "mmmyy")
        (this converts to month-year format)

Copy this formula down through row 4813.

Hit the F9 key to update your calculations.

In C2, type in the formula
        = TEXT(D2-31, "mmmyy")
        (this gives the previous month)

Copy this formula down through row 4813.

Hit the F9 key to update your calculations.

In A2, type in the formula
        = B2&E2
        (the & combines text together into one string)

Copy this formula down through row 4813.

Hit the F9 key to update your calculations.

We now need to create the Unique Key Code in the Bond_Tradings file. Since we will not be using the date codes in any formulas in the Bond_Tradings file, we can create this Unique Key Code formula in one sweep.

Actions:

Pull up the Bond_Tradings sheet

Insert a new column in the A Column

In A1, type the label "Key Code"

In A2, type the formula =TEXT(B2,"mmmyy")&D2
(combines mmyy date and cusip)

CHAPTER THREE

Flag The Securities and Assess Whether Traded Or Not

Using the Vlookup function and our new Unique Key Code, we will not determine if each security in the Bond_Holdings file has been traded that month or not.

Now, one limitation of Excel is that it will not read your answers in the A column when we use it with the Vlookup formula. (It will not see our resulting answer, meaning it will not see our Unique Key Code that we created).

Another limitation of the Vlookup function is that the A column must be sorted into ascending order. If not, the feature will not work properly.

Our strategy to determine whether traded or not will be to go record by record in the Bond_Holdings file. It will look at our Unique Key Code of month&year&cusip, and see if there is a similar Unique Key Code in the Bond_Trades file. If there is, then the "flag" will be "traded." If there is not, then you will get an error code #NA.

To make the spreadsheet less cumbersome, will put an If-Then statement in. This, combined with the ISERROR function, will allow us to put the correct flag in the cell if the error comes up. This If-Then will determine if the error code #NA comes up If it does, then the cell will have the flag "not traded".

Actions:

Pull up the Bond_Trades sheet.

Click on cell A2

Click on the Sort Button (AZ in the button bar)

Note: *This very important to sort the Unique Key Code column on the Bond_Trades sheet.*

Note: *If you feel you will need to return to the original order, you can put in a column called "Record Number." Put 1 and 2 in the first two cells, and drag down the*
handle on the cursor. This will allow you to later sort on this column and return it to the original order.

Pull up the Bond_Holdings sheet

Insert a new column at the B column

At B1, type in the label "Flag"

At B2, type in the formula

=IF(ISERROR(VLOOKUP(A2, Trades!$A$2:$B$2565, 2, FALSE)), "no trade", "trade")

Flag The Securities and Assess Whether Traded Or Not

Important: The Bond_Holdings sheet has 4813 records. The number of Vlookups we are implementing will greatly slow down the calculation process. We will do two things to offset this.

First, make the calculations <u>manual</u> instead of <u>automatic</u>. If this is not done, you will sit for a while as it frequently updates its calculations.

Actions:

Click on the Tools menu

Click on Options

Click on the Calculation tab

Click on Manual

Turn off the checkbox, Recalculate before Save

To update all calculations, hit the F9 key

The second thing we can do, is a process that keeps the data but removes the time consuming formulas. This is done by highlighting all of the data in the column, ***control + c*** to copy, go to a blank page in MS Word, ***control + v*** to paste it. Go back to Excel, hit the delete key to remove all the data that is now highlighted. Go back to MS Word, put the cursor back in your table. In the table menu, click Select Table. Click control + c to copy, go back to MS Excel to paste.

This 'cleanup' step is optional, but highly recommended.

This entire 'cleaning' process takes less than 15 seconds, but will save tons of time later when we start filling up our spreadsheet with many formulas. (This process can also be used in other situations when certain find/replace functions do not appear to be finding the results in any formulas.)

Important: Vlookups for all of our formulas

Again, due to the requirement of Vlookup functions that all the data in the first column must be sorted, it is strongly recommended to create an additional worksheet tab and copy the Bond_Holdings file to that sheet (and then sort the first column). [If you chose not to do it this way, then the first column in your Bond_Holdings file must always be sorted prior to doing a lookup.]

Actions:

Pull up the Holdings sheet

Create a second sheet called Holdings2

Copy all of the data from the Bond_Holdings sheet to the Holdings2 sheet

Click anywhere on the first column

Click on the Sort button

CHAPTER FOUR

Setup for Categories, Rate of Return, and Weights

We will be working with five categories of Rate of Return. We will build formulas to determine which of these categories each record will fall into. Each Category will have a different formula.

To make our work somewhat easier, we will insert eleven twelve columns (Category, ROR and Weight for each of the five categories, then a total for the ROR). It does not have to be done this way, but, without the split up the If-Then formulas become utterly outrageous and complex.

The five categories and their Rate of Return formulas are as follows.

Color codes: Field names in black are from the Bond_Holdings sheet.
Field names in green are from the Bond_Trades sheet.
Field names in dark red are calculated from formulas

Category 1
-_____   No trades

Category 1A - accrued income is lower than last month

ROR = (Total Value + Prior Month Accrued Income) / (Prior Month Total Value - (50% * Prior Month Accrued Income))

Category 1B - accrued income is equal to or greater than last month

ROR = (Total Value - Prior Month Total Value) / Prior Month Total Value

Category 2 - security is fully sold this month

ROR = (FirstMoney+Interest - Prior Month Total Value) / Prior Month Total Value

Category 3 - partial sale, the Currently Owned field is less than last month's Currently Owned ROR = (Total Value - Prior Month Total Value + FirstMoney+Interest) / (Prior Month Total Value * (FirstMoney+Interest * 50%))

Category 4 - new position purchase, the cusip did not exist in the previous month's list

ROR = (Total Value -FirstMoney+Interest) / (FirstMoney+Interest * 50%)

Category 5 - add-on to existing, Currently Owned field is greater than last month's

Currently Owned ROR = (Total Value - Prior Month Total Value - FirstMoney+Interest) / (Prior Month Total Value * (FirstMoney+Interest * 50%))

Category 6 - multiple trades bring us back to what we held the previous month

Actions:

Pull up the Holdings sheet

Go to the E Column

Insert eleven new columns starting with E1, label each cell as follows:

E1	F1	G1	H1	I1
Cat	ROR No Trades	Weight	ROR Full Scale	Weight

J1	K1	L1	M1	N1
ROR Reduced	Weight	ROR New Position	Weight	ROR Increased

O1	P1			
Weight	Monthly Total			

CHAPTER FIVE

Assessing The Category For Each Record

A. Important: error codes

These formulas will become very complex, very quickly. Do to the nature of our lookups, we will be getting a lot of errors. If the Unique Key Code and other data is not found in the Bond_Trades file, we get the #NA error. This #NA error, then produces other errors in any new formulas that is basing its calculations on these fields. Unfortunately, an error in one cell, can cause the entire formula to bomb out and produce an #NA result. (Even a simple =SUM(range) formula can bomb out if certain errors are found in the range.)

To filter out the lookups which produce an error, we again use a combination of the If-Then function with the ISERROR() function.

To ease the use of the If-Then and ISERROR combination, we will create the original formula. Then, we will copy it. Then, we will paste it within our If-Then and ISERROR formula. This saves a lot of typing, and helps you to avoid typing mistakes. (This will make a lot of sense as we continue on.)

B. Assessing the Category

Since Category one is already determined from a previous formula, we will use four If-Then statements, and then combine them into one for this Category column. Then, we will apply the above if-then/iserror functions.

You may wish to work on each of these formulas one at a time. If so, each formula is provided exactly as it would appear on your spreadsheet.

Then, later, you can copy and paste the massive nested If-Then statement which follows this section.

Category 2 - security is fully sold this month

> = if vlookup(Next Month Owned) causes an error, it means it was fully sold this month

Since we did not create a separate column for next month&yr, we will have to create this with another text statement and include this as part of our Vlookup statement.

If typed in separately (not within the nested statement, as we will do) this formula would be:

> =IF(ISERROR(VLOOKUP(TEXT(C2+31, "mmmyy")&S2, Holdings2!$A$2:$Q$4813, 13, FALSE)), "fully sold", "")

What this statement is saying is:

> a) let's create a Unique Key Code for next month   =
> TEXT(C2+31, "mmmyy")&S2

17

b) let's look up the currently Owned column for next month (column 13 in the vlookup)

c) if we get an error during this Vlookup, then the security must have been fully sold this month

Category 2 is an interesting one. This Category can be met, as well as the other categories. Meaning, it can be indicated as Fully Sold for next month, yet still be assessed as an Increase, Same or Decrease from the number owned in the previous month. Since we want only one Category, and Fully Sold status appears to supercede the other categories, we can put all of the If-Thens into a nested If-Then. The nested statement reads each If-Then in a sequence, one after the other.

Important: For the last month in our records, December98, the Vlookups will find no data for the following month. Per our formula, it will incorrectly interpret that this security is fully sold. We will go into these specific records for Dec98, and put in a different formula that does not have the "fully sold"

If-Then statement nested within it. Without this, it will go and assess these Dec98 records as one of the other 4 categories.

Category 3 - partial sale, the Currently Owned field is less than last month's Currently Owned

If typed in separately (not within the nested statement, as we will do) this formula would be:

if vlookup(Prev Month Owned) < vlookup(Owned) then it is "decreased"

=IF(VLOOKUP(D2&S2, Holdings2!$A$2:$Q$4813, 13, FALSE)>Z2, "decrease", "")

D2&S2 = combines prev month and cusip, to create a Unique Key Code for last month

Holdings2!$A$2:$Q$4813 = the dimensions of the table on the Holdings2 tab

I3 = column 13, gives you the number Owned for this month

Z2 = Owned field (currently owned, for this month)

FALSE = needed with every Vlookup command (else it returns next closest number)

Category 4 - new position purchase, the cusip did not exist in the previous month's list

= if vlookup(Prev Month Owned) causes an error, then it is "new purchase"

If typed in separately (not within the nested statement, as we will do) this formula would be:

= if (iserror(VLOOKUP(D2&S2, Holdings2!$A$2:$Q$4813, 13, FALSE)), "new purchase", "")

This statement is saying that if the Vlookup function causes an error, then it is assumed that this security is a new purchase. If there is no error, then "" would be displayed. We would want this statement to be our first statement in the nested If-Then statement.

Category 5 - add-on to existing, Currently Owned field is greater than last month's Currently Owned

> = if (Prev Month Owned > Owned) then it is
> "increased"
> If typed in separately (not within the nested statement, as we will do) this formula would be:
>
> =IF(VLOOKUP(D2&S2,Holdings2!$A$2:$Q$4813,13,FALSE)<z2,"increase","")

Category 6 - multiple trades bring us back to what we held the previous month

A sixth Category would be "is it the same as last month?", but none of our Rate of Return work appears to need this Category. This could mean that there were some trades, but they now equal the number owned from the previous month. We will work this option into the nested statement.

C. Creating The Nested If-Then Statement.

Now, we could have several columns, each with its own If-Then statement. This approach would present a problem. First, we have other formulas coming (namely the ROR formulas) which need to look over and see which Category the security falls under, then do a separate ROR calculation based on that specific category.

Buckle your seatbelt - this is going to be a loop-de-loop! This statement will incorporate all of the If-Then statements listed previously in assessing which Category the record falls into.. For reasons previously stated, we want the If-Then to flow in a specific order:

Category 2 - security is fully sold this month

Category 4 - new position purchase, the cusip did not exist in the previous month's list **Category 3** - partial sale, the Currently Owned field is less than last month's Currently Owned **Category 5** - add-on to existing, Currently Owned field is greater than last month's Currently Owned **Category 6** - multiple trades bring us back to what we held the previous month

The flow of logic will along these lines:

First If-Then:
Does the Unique Key Code exist next month? If answer is NO, then the category for this security is FULLY SOLD If the answer is YES, then go to the next If-Then

Second If-Then:
Does the Unique Key Code exist in the previous month? If the answer is NO, then the category for this security is NEW PURCHASE If the answer is YES, then go to the next If-Then

Third If-Then:
Is the current number owned less than last month? If the answer is NO, then go to the next If-Then

If the answer is YES, then the category for this security is DECREASE

Fourth If-Then:
Is the current number owned greater than last month?

If the answer is NO, then the category for this security is SAME

If the answer is YES, then the category for this security is INCREASE

At this point, we can end the string of If-Then statements. If it meets neither the 3rd or 4th in this list, obviously it is the same as last month, which means it is most likely on the No Trade list assessed in Part 5.

If not the case, then another option presents itself. Specifically, it could NOT be on the No Trade list, but, rather, it could have had two or more trades, and then wound up with the same number held as last month.

Our work at this point does not calculate the ROR on this type of trade action. You can indeed determine if this is the case if you have "SAME" as your category, yet, the assessment flag comes up as TRADED.

Now, accepting the point that we need to have one single column providing the Category assessment, let's turn to the task, and build the actual nested If-Then statement. We can refer above to the text which provides the actual formulas, if you were trying them out one at a time. These will be used in the nested statement. You will notice that if the statement is true, it returns the name of the category. If the statement is false, then, instead of returning the null by having the double quotes, we will put in the next If-Then statement along the sequence chain.

Actions:

Pull up the Bond_Holdings sheet go to the Category column, cell E2 copy and paste the following formula copy this formula down through row 4813.

Hit the F9 key to update your calculations.

=IF(ISERROR(VLOOKUP(TEXT(C2+31, "mmmyy")&R2, Holdings2!$A$2:$Q$4813, 13, FALSE)), "fully sold", IF(ISERROR(VLOOKUP(D2&R2, Holdings2!$A$2:$Q$4813, 13, FALSE)), "new purchase", IF(VLOOKUP(D2&R2, Holdings2!$A$2:$Q$4813, 13, FALSE)>Z2, "decrease", IF(VLOOKUP(D2&R2, Holdings2!$A$2:$Q$4813, 13, FALSE)<Z2, "increase", "same"))))

CHAPTER SIX

Determining The Rate Of
Return For No Trades

We will now be working with all of the ROR formulas. First on our list, the F Column, will be those which we screened early on, the No Trades flag.

All of our ROR formulas will begin the same way. We will look back to the Flag column and/or the Category column. Then, we will say if it is this type, then do this formula. The next ROR column will say, if it is the second type, then do the second formula. Seems a little much, but otherwise we are left with creating If-Then statements even larger than the one above.

Our ROR formula for No Trades will be more complex than the others, as it will require an additional If-Then statement determining if the Accrued Income for each record is lower or higher/equal than the previous month. It will calculate the ROR with separate formulas for either condition.

This ROR determination could be made into two columns due to this extra condition screening, but, might as well do it with one column.

Determining The Rate Of Return For No Trades

A. Writing The Formulas, Initial Components

If (Prev Month Accrued Income < curr month Accrued Income) then ROR = (Total Value + Prev Month Accrued Income) / (Prev Month Total Value - (Prev Month Accrued Income * 50%))

ELSE then ROR = (Total Value - Prev Month Total Value) / Prev Month Total Value

Let's break this down a little by individual formulas, then, we will combine them into the master formula.

You can try these out individually to verify they work.

First, the formula to lookup the **prev month Accrued Income** would be:

> =VLOOKUP(D2&R2, Holdings2!$A$3:$Q$4814, 15, FALSE)

> *row 15 is Accrued Income on the Holdings2 sheet*

Second, **curr month Accrued Income** is simply Column AA on the current sheet

Third, **curr month Total Value** is simply Column AB on the current sheet

Fourth, the formula to lookup the **prev month Total Value** would be:

> =VLOOKUP(D2&R2, Holdings2!$A$3:$Q$4814, 16, FALSE)

Excelling With Excel Formulas

row 16 is Total Value on the Holdings2 sheet
From this, we can calculate the two RORs

If Accrued Income from current month is less than previous month:

= (Total Value + Prev Month Accrued Income) / (Prev Month Total Value - (Prev Month Accrued Income * 50%))

(AB2 + VLOOKUP(D2&R2, Holdings2!$A$3:$Q$4814, 15, FALSE)) / (VLOOKUP(D2&R2, Holdings2!$A$3:$Q$4814, 16, FALSE) - (VLOOKUP(D2&R2, Holdings2!$A$3:$Q$4814, 15, FALSE) * 50%))

If Accrued Income from current month is equal or greater than previous month:

(Total Value - Prev Month Total Value) / Prev Month Total Value

(AB2 - VLOOKUP(D2&R2, Holdings2!$A$3:$Q$4814, 15, FALSE)) / VLOOKUP(D2&R2, Holdings2!$A$3:$Q$4814, 15,FALSE)

B. Laying The Groundwork For Our First ROR, Subcategorize The "No Trades"

To streamline our process someone, let's first build a cell that will subcategorize the "No Trades" category. This cell will compare the previous month's ACCRUED INCOME, against the current month's ACCRUED INCOME, and decide if it is (a) less than; (b)

26

greater than; or, (c) no record was found {for previous month by which to make our comparison}.

FIRST, create the formula to lookup the Previous Month's Accrued Income

As previously developed, our formula for calculating the Previous Month's Accrued Income depends on a vlookup of the Holdings2 sheet. [Keep in mind we cannot use the current sheet to perform this vlookup, as the first column in the data sheet must be sorted in ascending order for the vlookup to function properly.]

After inserting a column at the current fifth column (called "Cat: Prev Acc Inc to This Mo Acc Inc"), our vlookup formula is:

VLOOKUP(D2&S2,Holdings2!$A$3:$Q$4814,15,FALSE)

Explanation	Current Data
D2 is the cell containing the code for Prev Month	Feb97
S2 is the cell containing the Cusip	9999999$A
Column 15 contains the data for ACCRUED INCOME	No record found for Feb979999999$A
FALSE - means find and provide the exact match only (True would tell it to find the next closest)	--

SECOND, what if we get an error code?

If the above vlookup produces an error code, this means there was no record in the data table for that PrevMonth and Cusip. We will have to put the ISERROR statement first; then, if there is an error, it will return with "No Record."

THIRD, once the number is found, determine if the Accrued Income of the previous month is "less than" the Accrued Income of the current month. If not less than, then the category will be "equal / greater than". Once determined, return the category depending on the answer.

Summary:

1. Perform the lookup. Is there an error? If yes, answer is: "no record found"

2. Is the PrevMonth Accrued Income less than current month? If yes, answer is "less than" else answer is "equal / greater than"

Our formula for this column will be:

> =IF(ISERROR(VLOOKUP(D2&S2, Holdings2!$A$3:$Q$4814, 15, FALSE)), "nothing found", IF((VLOOKUP(D2&S2, Holdings2!$A$3:$Q$4814, 15, FALSE))<(VLOOKUP(C2&S2, Holdings2!$A$3:$Q$48 14, 15, FALSE)), "less than", "equal / greater than"))

C. Laying The Groundwork For Our First ROR, Calculating Vlookup Variables

To streamline all of our ROR formulas, let's insert a few columns that will contain the values needed in the RORs which are obtained by vlookups (vlookups return Previous Month fields). This will make the final ROR formulas much less complex.

Determining The Rate Of Return For No Trades

Referring back to the Item A in this Section, our formulas are:

Variable	Formula
Prev Month Accrued Income	=VLOOKUP(D2&S2, Holdings2!$A$3:$Q$4814, 15, FALSE)
Prev Month Total Value	=VLOOKUP(D2&R2, Holdings2!$A$3:$Q$4814, 16, FALSE)
Total Value	=AB2

We will want to put in an ISERROR statement, so that if no records are found, it will say such (instead of the confusing #NA statement).

Actions:

At the current G and column, let's insert two columns

At G1, type in the label	*Prev Month Acc Income*
At H1, type in the label	*Prev Month Total Value*
At G2, type in the formula	=IF(ISERROR(VLOOKUP($D2&$U2, Holdings2!$A$3:$Q$4814, 15, FALSE)), "nothing found", VLOOKUP($D2&$U2, Holdings2!$A$3:$Q$4814, 15, FALSE))

Copy this formula down through row 4813.

Hit the F9 key to update your calculations.

At H2, type in the formula

=IF(ISERROR(VLOOKUP($D2&$U2, Holdings2!$A$3:$Q$4814, 16, FALSE)), "nothing found", VLOOKUP($D2&$U2, Holdings2!$A$3:$Q$4814, 16, FALSE))

Copy this formula down through row 4813.

Hit the F9 key to update your calculations.

D. Calculating the ROR Based On the Subcategory

This is the only category which has two subcategories. Depending on the subcategory, there are two different formulas for determining the ROR. Because of this, we will use nested If-Then statements.

> If [category = "no trade"] and [subcategory = "less than"]
> THEN, calculate the ROR this way:
>
> (Total Value + Prev Month Accrued Income) / (Prev Month Total Value - (Prev Month Accrued Income * 50%))

With our two new columns, the actual formula for this subcategory will be:

> = (AB2 + G2) / (H2 - (G2 * 50%) =(AB2+G2)/(H2-(G2*50%))

Note: without the two new columns, our formula would be:

> = (AB2 + VLOOKUP(D2&S2, Holdings2!$A$3:$Q$4814, 15, FALSE)) / (VLOOKUP(D2&S2, Holdings2!$A$3:$Q$4814, 16, FALSE) - (VLOOKUP(D2&S2, Holdings2!$A$3:$Q$4814, 15, FALSE) * 50%))

> If [category = "no trade"] and [subcategory = "equal / greater than"]
>
> THEN, calculate the ROR this way:

(Total Value - Prev Month Total Value) / Prev Month Total Value

With our two new columns, the actual formula for this subcategory will be:

= (AB2 - H2) / H2 =(AB2-H2)/H2

E. Final Formula

With our two new columns, and, based on the above If-Then statements, the formula for the ROR column for No Trades will be:

=IF((B2="no trade")*(F2="less than"), (AB2+G2)/(H2-(G2*50%)), IF((F2="greater than")*(B2="no trade"), (AB2-H2)/H2, ""))

CHAPTER SEVEN

Determining The Monthly First Money Plus Interest

A. Combining Cusips Together For The First Money Plus Interest Variable

In calculating the remaining RORs, we will use another variable in our formulas, FirstMoneyPlusInterest. This data is not found on the Holdings spreadsheet, but it is on the Trades spreadsheet. Using our Key Code (Cusip+Date), let's perform a vlookup and put a column on our Holdings spreadsheet (just as before, this will simplify the formulas).

There are many trades for the same cusip each month. In calculating the FirstMoneyPlusInterest field, we will first have to group all the identical cusips together per month. For example, if *Walden Residential Properties* is traded five times, each of those five are combined together. The FirstMoneyPlusInterest field for that cusip is now the combined sum of all five trades.

We will insert a new spreadsheet tab, CombCusips for Bond_Trades file. We will sort the Trades file first by month, then by cusip. Then, we will apply a Subtotal to it, which will group any repeats and provide a sum total for the FirstMoneyPlusInterest variable. [There are 1109 records which have a repeat cusip code grouped in the same month.]

To make the work a little easier on this Bond_Trades file, I moved the FirstMoneyPlusInterest column to the second column.

Actions:

> Insert a new column at column B, named FirstMoneyPlusInterest
>
> Highlight all of column M, copy, and paste to column B
>
> When successful, delete column M

Now to work with the Subtotal feature that will group the monthly cusips, and provide you with the sums of the FirstMoneyPlusInterest field.

Actions:

> Click anywhere on the A column (KeyCode)
>
> Click on the AZ sort button
>
> Click on the Data Menu, click on Subtotal, make the following choices:
>
> At each change in: KeyCode
>
> Use Function: Sum
>
> Add Subtotal to: FirstMoneyPlusInterest
>
> Click ok

When the groupings are displayed, click on the [2] outline button for the groups [You will see 1, 2, 3 displayed at the top of all the plus signs on the far left of your page. From the original 2564 records originally displayed, we are now reduced to 1455 records (due to the repeated cusips in each monthly grouping)].

B. Sterilizing The Data After Performing The Subtotals Of The FirstMoneyPlus Interest Variable

Now, we want this data to be on a new spreadsheet for performing our vlookups, but, if we simply do a copy and paste to another spreadsheet, it brings along data that we do not want (try and see). What happens is that it brings along with it all of the other information from button 3 of the subtotal outline, even though we clicked on and copied only the data from button 2 of the subtotal outline. This extra data would make our future ROR tasks inoperable since it would be pulling up the first hit matching the key code and not pulling up the total of several key codes which we group and subtotal. So, before copying and pasting it to another sheet, we want to "sterilize" it first.

I found that by copying it to MS Word, then, copying it from MS Word back to Excel, it cleans out and removes all of the data that comes with it hidden inside when you attempt a normal copy and paste. As mentioned much earlier, this process is great for vlookups, as well. (If you do a repeated vlookups - and the data will never change again after that initial vlookup is performed - do the process with Word and you will not have to wait while all of your vlookups are updated. If you have several columns of vlookups and several thousand rows, as we do in this scenario, it takes a lot of time to update all of those.)

Actions:

> Insert a new sheet, called CombCusips, go back to the Bond_Trades sheet highlight A1 through B4021, click Control + C (performs a copy)
>
> Pull up a blank MS Word document, click Control + V (performs a paste) After the paste, click back on the table (the cursor jumped past the table) Click on the Table Menu, click Select Table Click copy
>
> Go back to Excel, click on the CombCusips tab
>
> Paste the table from MS Word, to Excel
>
> Perform a Search/Replace, remove " Total" from this sheet (space in front of Total) by doing the search for Total and the replace with nothing
>
> Go to the Trades tab, and turn off Subtotal feature:
>
> Data menu, subtotals, click Remove All

C. Performing The Vlookups Based On The Data

We will now go back to our Bond_Holdings sheet, and perform a vlookup based on this newly compiled data for the FirstMoneyPlusInterest column.

Our regular vlookup formula would look like this:

> =VLOOKUP(A2, CombCusips!$A$2:$B$1456, 2, FALSE)

Item	Explanation
A2	Contains the Key Code (date + cusip)
CombCusips!$A$2:$B$1456	The table for our new subtotaled FirstMoneyPlusInterest column
2	The column for the actual FirstMoneyPlusInterest data
FALSE	Must be exact match of lookup

As usual, we want to attach the ISERROR codes so that we do not get the NA# errors. We can either leave them blank (which looks nicer), or, we can have it say "nothing found". This formula is given in the Actions statement following…

Actions:

Go to the G column, for our new FirstMoneyPlusInterest column

In G2, type in the vlookup formula:

=IF(ISERROR(VLOOKUP(A2, CombCusips!$A$2:$B$1456, 2, FALSE)), "nothing found", VLOOKUP(A2, CombCusips!$A$2:$B$1456, 2, FALSE))

Then, copy this formula down through row 4813.

Hit F9 to update your calculations.

CHAPTER EIGHT

Calculating The Rate Of Return For The Reduced Category

We have now set up several columns to serve as shortcuts in calculating the remaining ROR. We will be using these variables in different ways, so here is our list:

Variable name	Cell reference in our initial formula
TotalValue	AF2
PriorMoTotalValue	I2
FirstMoneyPlusInterest	G2

This, as you can imagine, will greatly reduce the length of our formulas. The initial run of this document did not include this step, and the formulas ended up being over 255 characters in length (with the multiple vlookups), and very hard to understand as well as revise.

As a quick sidebar, here is an example of the previous format:

```
= (AB2 + VLOOKUP(D2&S2,
Holdings2!$A$3:$Q$4814, 15, FALSE)) /
(VLOOKUP(D2&S2, Holdings2!$A$3:$Q$4814, 16,
FALSE) - (VLOOKUP(D2&S2,
Holdings2!$A$3:$Q$4814, 15, FALSE) * 50%))
```

Now, let's get the Rate of Return formulas for the Reduced category out of the way.

We will look to see if the Category is "decrease." If the If-Then meets the criteria, we will calculate the Rate of Return as follows:

> ROR = (TotalValue - PriorMoTotalValue + FirstMoneyPlusInterest) / (PriorMoTotalValue - (50% * FirstMoneyPlusInterest))

Per our current spreadsheet, the cell addresses with this formula can be substituted as follows:

> =(AF2 - I2 + G2) / (I2 - (50% * G2))
>
> =(AF2-I2+G2)/(I2-(50%*G2))

To avoid the problems associated with errors, we need to again combine this with the ISERROR statement. If we do not take the extra time to do this now, then our ROR totals will have errors. (It cannot add up a sum statement with the #VALUE! error anywhere in the row.

This statement will now look like this:

> =IF(ISERROR((AF2-I2+G2)/(I2-(50%*G2))),"",(AF2-I2+G2)/(I2-(50%*G2)))

Now, we need to attach the If-Then that determines if this is the "Reduced" category.

The statement will now look like this:

> =IF(E2="decrease", IF(ISERROR((AF2-I2+G2)/(I2(50%*G2))), "", (AF2-I2+G2)/(I2-(50%*G2))), "")

Actions:

Go to row cell N2, type in the above formula:

=IF(E2="decrease", IF(ISERROR((AF2-I2+G2)/(I2-(50%*G2))), "", (AF2-I2+G2)/(I2-(50%*G2))), "")

Copy that down through row 4813.

Hit the F9 key to update your calculations.

CHAPTER NINE

Calculating The Rate Of Return
For The Increased Category

Now, let's get the Rate of Return for the Increased category formulas out of the way.   We will look to see if the Category is "increase". If the If-Then meets the criteria, we will calculate the Rate of Return as follows:

ROR = (TotalValue - PriorMoTotalValue – FirstMoneyPlusInterest) / (PriorMoTotalValue + (50% * FirstMoneyPlusInterest))

Per our current spreadsheet, the cell addresses with this formula can be substituted as follows:

ROR = (AF2-I2-G2)/(I2+(50%*G2))

To avoid the problems associated with errors, we need to again combine this with the ISERROR statement. If we do not take the extra time to do this now, then our ROR totals will have errors. (It cannot add up a sum statement with the #VALUE! error anywhere in the row.

This statement will now look like this:

=IF(ISERROR((AF2-I2-G2)/(I2+(50%*G2))), "", (AF2-I2-G2)/(I2+(50%*G2)))

Calculating The Rate Of Return For The Increased Category

Now, we need to attach the If-Then that determines if this is the "Increased" category. The statement will now look like this:

=IF(E2="increase", IF(ISERROR((AF2-I2-G2)/(I2+(50%*G2)))),"", (AF2-I2-G2)/(I2+(50%*G2)))),"")

Actions:

Go to row cell R2 under the "ROR INCREASED" column, type in the above formula:

=IF(E2="decrease", IF(ISERROR((AF2-I2+G2)/(I2-(50%*G2)))), "", (AF2-I2+G2)/(I2-(50%*G2)))), "")

Copy that down through row 4813.

Hit the F9 key to update your calculations.

CHAPTER TEN

Calculating The Rate Of Return For The New Purchase Category

Now, let's get the Rate of Return for the New Position category formulas out of the way.

We will look to see if the Category is "new purchase". If the If-Then meets the criteria, we will calculate the Rate of Return as follows:

ROR = (TotalValue - FirstMoneyPlusInterest) / (50% * FirstMoneyPlusInterest)

Per our current spreadsheet, the cell addresses with this formula can be substituted as follows:

= (AF2 - G2) / (50% * G2))

= (AF2-G2)/(50%*G2)

To avoid the problems associated with errors, we need to again combine this with the ISERROR statement. If we do not take the extra time to do this now, then our ROR totals will have errors. (It cannot add up a sum statement with the #VALUE! error anywhere in the row.

This statement will now look like this:

> = IF(ISERROR((AF2-G2)/(50%*G2)), "", (AF2-G2)/(50%*G2))

Now, we need to attach the If-Then that determines if this is the "new purchase" category.

The statement will now look like this:

> =IF(E2="new purchase", IF(ISERROR((AF2-G2)/(50%*G2)),"",(AF2-G2)/(50%*G2)),"")

Actions:

> Go to row cell R2 under the "ROR NEW POSITION" column, type in the above formula:
>
> =IF(E2="new purchase", IF(ISERROR((AF2-G2)/(50%*G2)),"",(AF2-G2)/(50%*G2)),"")
>
> Copy that down through row 4813. Hit the F9 key to update your calculations.

CHAPTER ELEVEN

Calculating The Rate Of Return For The Full Sale Category

A. Creating A New Key Code For The Full Sale Records

This leaves us with the final category, "Fully Sold." This particular category presents some interesting problems.

Based on the text outlining the problem, we take it as a given that the Rate of Return for the Fully Sold should be calculated in the month in which there exists no units. This means that if in July, we look back and see that, yes, indeed, there were units existing in June, then, the ROR for that particular cusip is calculated in July.

The problem arises that, if the units are sold, then they will not show up in the Bond_Holdings sheet in July. Therefore, what we must do is create a new sheet, extract out the fully sold items, and replace them into the following month so that they can be grouped under that month for totaling the ROR, Weights and Overall monthly ROR.

This will be a tricky abstract process, but it is the last hard one. After this, it is nearly almost all done hill and the overall process is complete.

Well, at this point, we have already built formulas that determined if the current cusip was sold next month. As you may recall, this thought process was along the lines that if a cusip existed in one month, but, a vlookup reveals that it did not exist in the very next month, then it was sold either by one trade or a series of trades. We will use this category, and change the KeyCode to reflect the next month, then put that back in with the modified KeyCodes.

First, we create a new tab spreadsheet to work on, called "FullSale". Then, we sort all of the records by category on the Bond_Holdings sheet. We then copy out those records which are under the category of "fully sold", and place them on the new "FullSale" tab sheet. There are 413 of these records.

We then give these particular records a KeyCode (date + cusip) with the next month as the date!

Actions:

> Create a new tab sheet, called "FullSale"
>
> Go back to the Bond_Holdings sheet, and sort the Category column Scroll down to the "fully sold" categories (records 1146 - 1558)
>
> Select and CUT these records; past them over to the new "FullSale" tab sheet Insert a new column at Column B
>
> Type in the formula which will increase the KeyCode to the next month:
>
> =TEXT(V2+30, "mmmyy")&W2

Excelling With Excel Formulas

Copy this down from row 2, through row 414.

Hit the F9 key to update your calculations

Now, we need to perform the sterilizing function we did earlier (copy to MS Word, and back to Excel again). This will give us nice clean text that is not based on any formulas.

Actions:

Highlight b2 through b414, copy, and paste onto a blank MS Word document

Click on the table now in the MS Word document

Click Table menu, click select table, click copy

Go back to Excel, click on cell A2, click paste

Delete the B column

Take a quick minute to scroll down from B2 through B10. Notice each new cell reveals the formula? However, scroll down from A2 through A10 and we see that we now have clean text with no formula. This makes sure our lookups are accurate, and also saves time in not requiring continual calculation time.

Lets put these back into our original Bond_Holdings sheet.

Actions:

Go to FullSale sheet

Highlight A2 through I414, click copy

Go to the original Bond_Holdings sheet

46

Go to cell A1146 (this should be your first blank cell), click paste

B. Calculating The Rate Of Return

Now, let's get the Rate of Return for the Full Sale category formulas out of the way.

We will look to see if the Category is "fully sold". If the If-Then meets the criteria, we will calculate the Rate of Return as follows:

ROR = (FirstMoneyPlusInterest - PriorMoTotalValue) / PriorMoTotalValue

Per our current spreadsheet, the cell addresses with this formula can be substituted as follows:

= (G2 - AF2) / AF2

= (G2-AF2)/AF2

To avoid the problems associated with errors, we need to again combine this with the ISERROR statement. If we do not take the extra time to do this now, then our ROR totals will have errors. (It cannot add up a sum statement with the #VALUE! error anywhere in the row.

This statement will now look like this:

=IF(ISERROR((G2-AF2)/AF2),"",(G2-AF2)/AF2)

Now, we need to attach the If-Then that determines if this is the "fully sold" category.

The statement will now look like this:

=IF(E2="fully sold", IF(ISERROR((G2-AF2)/AF2),"",(G2-AF2)/AF2),"")

Actions:

Go to row cell L2 under the "ROR FULLY SOLD" column, type in the above formula:

=IF(E2="fully sold", IF(ISERROR((G2-AF2)/AF2),"",(G2-AF2)/AF2),"")

Copy that down through row 4813. Hit the F9 key to update your calculations.

CHAPTER TWELVE

Calculating The Weights

A. Preparing The Field Called: ALLPriorMoTotalValue

At last, our final step, calculating the weights and the High Yield Monthly Return!

The formula for calculating the weights is:

Weight = ROR * (PriorMoTotalValue / ALLPriorMoTotalValue)

The field called ALLPriorMoTotalValue is a sum total of ALL Total Values for that month. Before proceeding any further, we will have to compile a new sheet with a table of this information. We can then create another column with vlookups referring to this new table.

Actions:

Create a new tab sheet, called "AllPMTotalValue"

Go to the Bond_Holdings sheet

Copy cells A1 through I4813

Cleanse the data, by copying to MS Word, and back to the "AllPMTotalValue" sheet

Delete columns D through H

Sort on the C column, DateCode, in ascending order

Perform a subtotal function

At each change in	= DateCode
Use Function	= Sum
Add subtotal to	= PrevMonthTotalVal

Delete columns A and B

Highlight and copy this entire table to a blank page in MS Word

Go back to Excel, hit the Escape key to clear the selection

Remove the subtotals: data menu, subtotals, remove all

Delete all of this information from this "AllPMTotalValue"tab sheet

Go back to MS Word, click on the table, click on the Table menu, Select Table

We now have a table that can be used for to calculate the weights with vlookup formulas.

Now, we can refer back to this table with vlookups inside of the weight calculations (4 columns times 4000 rows is a lot of vlookups that will slow down your calculations), or, we can do as before and pop these into a new column (let's do that!).

B. Preparing A New Column, ALLPriorMoTotalValue

The vlookups do not seem to want to perform very well on this new table since the first column in the table is all dates. For some reason, vlookup just does not like to perform with dates. I found that if you trick the software, by changing the dates into some other form of full text, it works fine. You can then combine the actual vlookup criteria with another phony word.

In our scenario, we conveniently have the word " Total" immediately following our dates on the table we will perform the vlookups with. This also prevents Excel from changing this column into the dreaded date format (which, in turn, prevents vlookup from performing).

So, now, lets create a vlookup formula that incorporates the word " Total" in it. Very easy to do:

Instead of using just C2 in our vlookup formula, we will use:

C2&" Total"

We find that this now works exceptionally well.

So, our formula in J2 will now be:

=VLOOKUP(C2&" Total",
AllPMTotalValue!$A$2:$B$23, 2, FALSE)

Actions:

Go to the Bond_Holdings tab sheet

Go to the J column, insert a new column, call it "All PMTV"

Type in the above formula

Copy this down through row 4813

Click F9 to update the calculations

To reduce calculation time for this particular column, you can copy this column out to MS Word, and back in again.

This will knock off the time consuming vlookup formulas for this column.

C. Calculating The Weights

To reduce calculation time for this particular column, you can copy this column out to MS Word, and back in again.

This will knock off the time consuming vlookup formulas for this column.

We will prepare our formula in such a way that we can copy it across, and then down.

As stated above, weights are calculated as follows:

Weight = ROR * (PriorMoTotalValue / ALLPriorMoTotalValue)

Based on our current spreadsheet, this formula in L2 would be:

Calculating The Weights

=K2*(I2/J2)

We will put dollar signs in front of the I2 and the J2, to anchor those columns so we can copy across.

We want to put the ISERROR statement here, so that a zero appears if there is an error. (If we put in a blank cell, as we have always done in the past, then, we will get the #VALUE error, even if it only finds one such blank cell, when adding a row of cells.)

Actions:

Go to L2 and enter in our first formula:

=IF(ISERROR(K2*($I2/$J2)),"0",K2*($I2/$J2))

Click on copy

Go to N2, click paste

Go to P2, click paste

Go to R2, click paste

Go to T2, click paste

(You can look back at each of these, and see that the formulas are indeed correct; we can now copy them down) go back to L2, copy down to row 4813

Go back to N2, copy down to row 4813

Go back to P2, copy down to row 4813

Go back to R2, copy down to row 4813

53

Go back to T2, copy down to row 4813

Now, click on the column headings for columns L, N, P, R, T while holding CTRL key

With all these Weight columns highlighted, click on Format menu, click on cells menu

Click Number category, change decimal places to 7

Click the F9 key to update the calculations (and go grab some coffee during the wait!)

D. Calculating Monthly Sums Of The Weights

We now will sum up each of these columns, then, do a subtotal grouping to calculate the monthly subtotals. This, then, will be the long sought after High Yield Monthly return (approximation).

Actions:

Go to the U column, called "ROR Total"

Type in the formula, =L2+N2+P2+R2+T2

Copy this down to row 4813

E. Calculating The High Yield Monthly Return
Actions:

Perform a subtotal function to group by month.

At each change in	= DateCode
Use function	= SUM
Add subtotal to	= ROR Total

Go to the upper left corner (where you see 1,2,3) and click 2. With the subtotals reduced to monthly values, copy and paste this data to a new sheet.

Highlight c200 through U4836, copy, paste this to a new MS Word document.

You will need to delete 14 columns of this MS Word table, about 5 - 7 at a time.

Now, there it is! This is what we have been working towards! Here is the Rate of Return for the Bond Debenture Fund:

	Month	**Rate of Return**
1.	Mar-Year1 Total	0.0000000
2.	Apr-Year1 Total	(0.0003298)
3.	May-Year1 Total	0.0021872
4.	Jun-Year1 Total	0.0009276
5.	Jul-Year1 Total	0.0026328
6.	Aug-Year1 Total	0.0000076
7.	Oct-Year1 Total	0.0108293
8.	Nov-Year1 Total	0.0033626
9.	Dec-Year1 Total	0.0125351
10.	Jan-Year2 Total	0.0154752
11.	Feb-Year2 Total	0.0011098
12.	Mar-Year2 Total	0.0008144
13.	Apr-Year2 Total	0.0103252
14.	May-Year2 Total	0.0056731
15.	Jun-Year2 Total	0.4839753
16.	Jul-Year2 Total	0.6667920
17.	Aug-Year2 Total	0.6225463
18.	Sep-Year2 Total	0.7385662
19.	Nov-Year2 Total	0.7182493
20.	Dec-Year2 Total	0.0000000

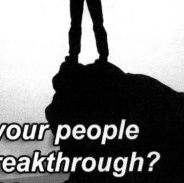

Isn't it time that your people enjoyed a major breakthrough? Experience this with Rick Saldan's Motivational Magic

Rick Wants to Help You and Your People!

Rick has spoken to many audiences around the United States bringing an energizing message of inspiration. He loves to help people find their hidden gifts and strengths, and shows them how to activate them.

Rick teaches people how to not only face their adversities and fears, but to allow difficulties to propel them further than they could go otherwise. He shows people how setbacks become stepping stones to something greater.

Rick has countless true life examples of harsh adversities that were funneled and leveraged to help him grow. Your people will be inspired to do the same, and no longer be held back from living and working to their fullest potential.

Imagine smashing through the barriers holding you back! Experience this with Rick Saldan's Motivational Magic

Rick's primary keynote message, *"Secrets for Accomplishing the Impossible"* is a high energy and fast paced presentation that is guaranteed to energize and keep your people on the edge of their seats. This is a powerful motivational event that your people will talk about for months to come. If you want your next special event to be truly spectacular, you'll want to invite Rick out to make your day more magical. You'll find Rick's Motivational Magic to be one of the most uniquely creative and inspiring programs available.

Rick impacts your audience with powerful visual effects, followed by content rich educational sessions, astounding true life inspiring stories and motivational messages. All designed to create an atmosphere that helps your people break through the barriers blocking them from their greatest accomplishments.

Learn 9 methods for gaining Freedom From Fear Forever! Experience this with Rick Saldan's Motivational Magic

The combined impact carries an intense emotional surge that creates the desire to step up and take action. Why is this important? Rick says, "I have been to countless seminars and conferences over the years.

Within 3 days, participants have forgotten 90% of what they were taught. By creating an emotional surge, what you are teaching becomes imprinted in their minds. The rate of retention and application now increases dramatically! Participants become committed to taking action that will have impact."

Your conference participants will say, "Rick was one of the best speakers we have ever had." To hire Rick Saldan for your special event, visit his website at:

www.MotivationalMagic.com